TopReaders

Mummies

Robert Coupe

Contents

Ancient Egyptians made dead bodies into mummies to preserve them. Some bodies become mummies by accident.

The God-kings

Rulers in ancient Egypt were called pharaohs. People believed that pharaohs were god-kings. They thought these rulers could control how the River Nile flowed and how crops grew.

Egypt

Egypt is in northeast Africa. The Nile is a river that flows northward through Egypt into the Mediterranean Sea.

The Nile, Egypt

Visitors knelt down and kissed the ground to honor the pharaoh.

Egyptian Gods

The ancient Egyptians worshipped many gods. They believed that the god Horus controlled the land of Egypt. The pharaoh, then, was Horus in the form of a human being.

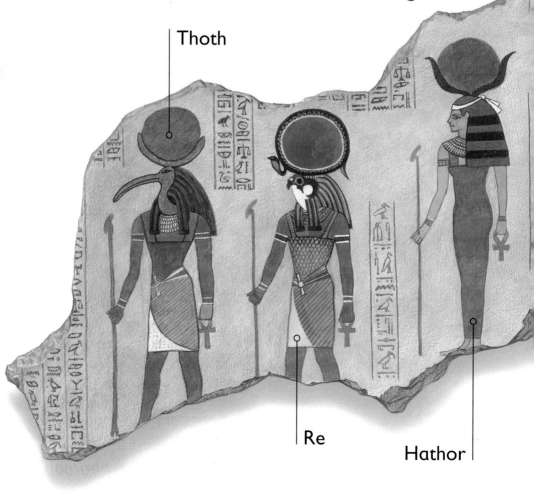

Thoth

Re

Hathor

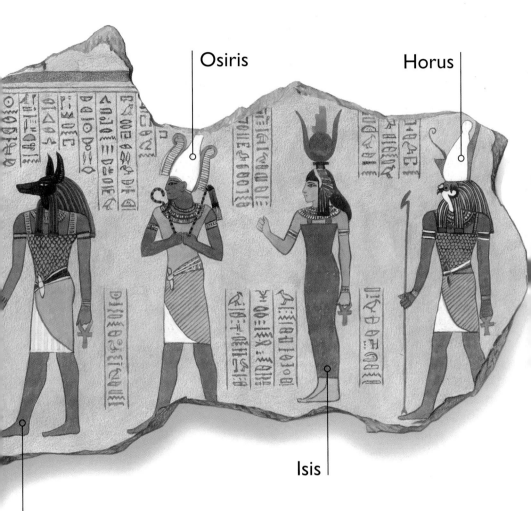

Osiris

Horus

Anubis

Isis

In this Egyptian wall painting, several gods are shown as humans with animals' heads. Horus has a falcon's head.

The Afterlife

Osiris was the Egyptian god of the dead.
If a person had led a good life,
their soul could live with
Osiris in the Afterlife.

This painting, on the wall of a tomb, is called the Book of the Dead. *It shows gods leading a dead person toward Osiris, who is seated on the right.*

Mummies

If a person's body did not decay, their soul could live forever. For almost 3,000 years, Egyptians believed this and made mummies of their dead. They put them in painted coffins.

wrapped mummy with mask

bottom of outer mummy case

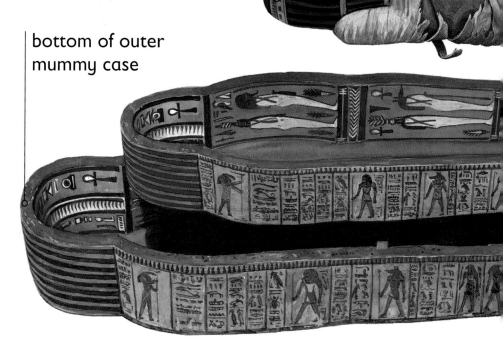

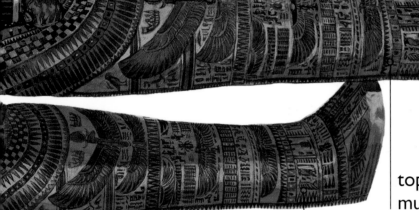

top of outer
mummy case

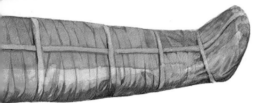

top of inner
mummy case

bottom of inner
mummy case

Mummies were wrapped in linen sheets, and then placed inside wooden or papier-mâché coffins, painted with pictures of gods.

Making a Mummy

To make a mummy, a dead body was dried out. This prevented it from rotting. The liver, lungs, stomach, and intestines were taken out. They were put into coffins called canopic jars.

Cat Mummy

Sometimes, cats were made into mummies. They were buried in special animal cemeteries near temples. They were not pets. The mummies were offerings to the gods.

A priest controlled the making
of a mummy. He wore a mask like
a jackal's head in honor of the god
Anubis, the god of mummy-making.

Buried with the Mummy

Egyptians used gold and colored stones to make jewelry for the rich. When people died, their jewelry and other possessions were buried with them. They believed they could use them in the Afterlife.

Fact File

There was plenty of gold in Egypt. Gold was mined in the desert and in Nubia, to the south. Silver was rarer. So it was more expensive.

The pharaoh Tutankhamen wore this amulet to protect him from evil. This piece of jewelry was buried with him.

chest containing
canopic jars

mummy

A Pharaoh's Funeral

At the funeral of a pharaoh, the mummy,
in its coffins, was placed on a large sledge.
It was pulled across the desert to a tomb.
Some tombs were cut deep into desert cliffs.

When the sledge reached the River Nile, it was pulled onto a barge, which took it to the other side of the river.

Cattle were taken to the tomb and sacrificed.

Mourners pulled the mummy on a sledge.

Fact File

Robbers often broke into tombs. That is why pharaohs' tombs were built in hidden places.

Tutankhamen

In 1922, British archeologist Howard Carter found the tomb of the pharaoh Tutankhamen. The mummy was almost 3,300 years old. A gold mask covered the mummy's face.

Tutankhamen

Tutankhamen was about **19** years old when he died. The picture on the left shows the face of his mummy. The other picture shows what he probably looked like.

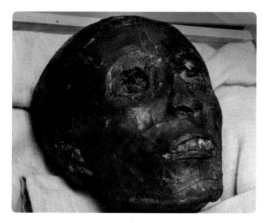

mummy

in real life

Museums

Egyptian mummies and their coffins are on display in many museums. The Cairo Museum in Egypt displays objects from Tutankhamen's tomb.

Queen Nefertiti

Nefertiti was the wife of Akhenaten, a pharaoh who lived more than 3,000 years ago. This statue of her is in a museum in Berlin, Germany.

Child Mummies

In 1972, in northwest Greenland, a grave was found. In it were the preserved bodies of five people. One was a baby. Another was a young boy. The others were adult women.

Where They Were

The bodies were buried under a covering of rock. This protected them from snow and rain. The cold, dry conditions preserved the bodies and their clothing.

Qilakitsok, Greenland

This is the mummified body of a six-month-old baby. This baby died and was buried more than 500 years ago.

Tollund Man

In 1950, two men were digging peat in a bog in Denmark. They were amazed to find a man's body. It had a rope around its neck. The man had been hanged more than 2,000 years earlier.

Where It Was

In ordinary soils, skin and flesh decay. But the acid in some peat bogs helps preserve bodies. Many other "peat bog" bodies have been found.

Tollund, Denmark

Ice Man

More than 5,000 years ago a man froze to death high in the Ötztal Alps . In 1991, two hikers found his body. It was perfectly preserved. It did not decay because wind dried it out and then it was covered with ice.

This is the oldest preserved human body that has yet been found. Even parts of its clothing were preserved on the body.

Where It Was

This mummy is usually called the Ice Man. But many people call it Ötzi, after the mountains where the hikers found it.

Ötztal Alps, Italy

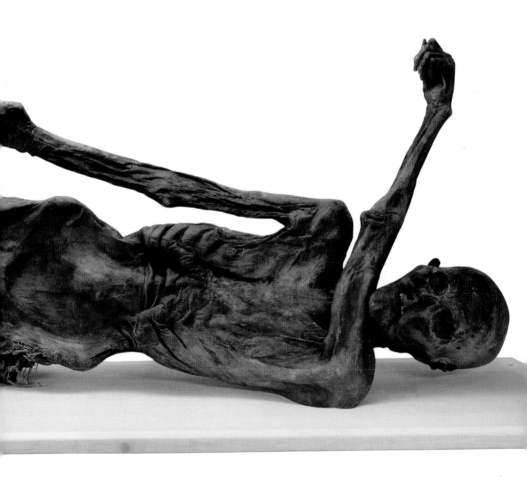

The Capuchin Catacombs

In Palermo, Italy, there is a strange museum. Beneath an old monastery , people can see thousands of mummies. The earliest one is of a monk who was mummified in 1599. One of the last is of a little girl who died in 1920.

Where They Are

Palermo is the largest city on the island of Sicily, at the south of Italy. Capuchins are monks. Catacombs are underground tombs with many bodies in them.

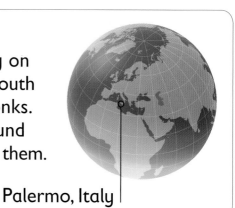

Palermo, Italy

At first, only monks were preserved in Palermo. Later, rich people paid to have their bodies made into mummies.

Quiz

Can you unscramble the words and match them with the right pictures?

TUAMEL

ACT MYMUM

RINTEFITE

MNAKTNHUAET

Glossary

amulet: a piece of jewelry that was worn to protect a person against evil

archeologist: a person who finds and studies objects from the distant past

canopic jars: containers where the organs of mummified bodies were stored in ancient Egypt

intestines: tubes inside the body through which the food that people eat moves, and where it is stored

linen: a strong cloth made from the fibers of flax plants

monastery: a place where religious people live together

monk: a religious man who lives, or lived, in a monastery with other religious men

mummified: made into a mummy, or turned into a mummy as a result of natural events

Nubia: the ancient country directly south of ancient Egypt. Today, Sudan is where Nubia used to be.

Ötztal Alps: part of the European Alps along the border of Austria and Italy

papier-mâché: a light, hard material made from paper that is soaked in water and then mixed with glue

peat: a soft, dark brown substance formed by decaying leaves, roots, and grasses. It is often used as heating fuel.

pharaohs: rulers in ancient Egypt

Index